Copyright page

Book Title: Born To Achieve
Book Sub-title: Living in Pursuit of Greatness
Author & Publish Name: Michael T. Brown

Copyright © 2012

Michael T. Brown

All rights reserved. Except as permitted under U.S. Copyright Act of 1976, no part of this publication may be reproduced, distributed, or transmitted in any form or by any means, or stored in a database or retrieval system, without the prior written permission of the publisher.

Publishers address and contact information
Visit our website at www.Brownsleadership.com.

ISBN-13: 978-0-578-10243-6

Printed in the United States of America

Book Design by: InstantPublishing.com
Photos by: Annie Malloy
Editing by: Michael T. Brown & Lovelle Golden

First Edition: February 2012

Michael T. Brown © Born to Achieve, 2012

To Donna, Thanks for serving our community which such honor and integrity. Stay strong, Michael

Dedication & Special Acknowledgements

This book is dedicated to you Lord. Thank You for being my everything, with You all things are possible.

To my wife Gilette and son Kaden, thank you for being a consistent source of love and support.

To my parents James T. & Audrey C. Brown, thank you for being their for myself and my siblings and for overcoming many of life's obstacles.

To my sisters and brothers, extended and church family, and friends, thank you for being the special individuals that you are. The strength thru love that you have shown me, has been immeasurable.

This book is also dedicated to my Grandparents. Although I have no memories of you, your spirit and legacy continues to impact me to this day. James & Louise Brown, Charlie & Georgia Crump...Rest in Peace.

Thank you Mrs. Annie Malloy for the wonderful illustrations that you provided for this project. Your genorisity and creativity are greatly appreciated.

A special thank you to Brother Lovelle Golden. Your extraordinary editing and proofreading skills helped take this project to the next level. I truly appreciate your insight, commitment and dedication.

To every person that has ever shared their story of struggle, pain and triumph with me; you have taught me and you have inspired me. To every young person still searching to find your way, this book is also dedicated to you.

Contents

Introduction	1
1 Education: The Key that Unlocks the Door	5
2 Character Matters	12
3 Family Matters	27
4 Career Planning	40
5 Strengthen your Spiritual Core	50
6 The Highly Effective Leader	57

Introduction

You were born to achieve. I believe this to be true for every individual, once each person is awakened to the potential for greatness that lies inside. Have you ever had the feeling that greatness was right at your fingertips, the feeling of being pregnant with possibilities, coupled with a boundless desire to reach your destiny? If so, you have come across the right book, at the right time. The purpose of this book is to empower, inform and inspire you the reader to grasp the opportunities for greatness that lie in front you.

About three years ago, I began taking note of a successful pastor, teacher, entrepreneur and author from the Chicago area, by the name of Dr. Bill Winston. Through his nationally syndicated television show, Dr. Winston spoke powerful truths and taught important life principles for success that resonated within me. Dr. Winston in his own unique way delivers these messages in such a manner that leaves his viewing and reading audience feeling more empowered and confident about pursuing their passion and purpose in life. Dr. Winston exudes confidence without coming across as arrogant; this confidence seems to transfer over to others.

I highlight this example of personal inspiration with the hope that the principles outlined in this book inspire you to pursue greatness like never before. Why this book and why now? Never before has our nation and the world at large been in such desperate need of its citizens to begin positioning ourselves to solve the critical problems that we face. These problems will continue to go unsolved unless more individuals step up and deliver. Our nation has some heavy lifting to do in order to improve its educational systems, its family structures and its governing institutions. We also need personal restoration if we are going to begin to solve the problems that ail us, problems such as the high drop-out rate of American students, high unemployment, crowded prisons, and the leadership vacuum in our society. This book will provide some insight and guiding principles for those who seek solutions.

At the time I came across the messages of Dr. Winston, I was at an interesting place in my life; I was ready to shift from the ordinary into the extraordinary and live out my full purpose and destiny. I had experienced setbacks and successes, and reached some semblance of fulfillment both personally and professionally. However, I could tell that there was much more for me to achieve. I was looking for more, longing to make a major impact with my life. Perhaps you find yourself at a similar juncture in your life; not satisfied with where you are and hungry to go to the next level of success and influence; intent on leaving a positive and lasting legacy. Although I have never met Dr. Winston personally, I felt the impact of his work and teachings thousands of miles away.

Everyone needs encouragement, it never gets old, and with the necessary tools and skills, individuals can begin the process of reaching their full potential. Are you a teenager (or adult) who is struggling to find your place in life, or have you become disillusioned with your current set of circumstances? Perhaps you have found success and meaning in life, but you are seeking out additional nuggets of wisdom to empower you in your journey towards greatness; stay tuned, this book is for you!

As a school and in-home counselor, I've had the privilege and opportunity to work with many adolescent youth, assisting them in reaching their academic, personal, and career goals. Not once, have I met a young person (or adult) that set out to fail. Success was the goal for each one. For many, somewhere along the line, their lives were interrupted with painful or difficult circumstances that hindered them from reaching their goals. Others lacked the guiding principles or role models that lead to successful living. I know what it is like to have the drive and motivation to reach your destiny, but lack the tools and or resources to make these dreams a reality.

The spring of 2011 is often referred to as the Arab Spring. Young people (and some old) took to the streets and made their voices heard as they demanded freedom for themselves and for their nation. These young people took their freedom into their own hands refusing to continue with the status quo of oppression and the legacy that ineffective leadership imposes. I encourage you to make your voice heard and grab hold of these guiding principles that follow in <u>Born to Achieve</u>. When individuals awaken to potential for greatness that lie inside of them, their lives, their families and our country's institutions will get the desired makeover and restoration that is so greatly needed.

Everyone was born to achieve. You were born with this desire. You didn't ask for it, it's your birthright. Sometimes the issues and problems of life can diminish the desire to achieve greatness. The concept of reaching greatness can be a very broad term and can have different meanings for different people, depending upon one's beliefs, goals and desires. I define *greatness* as – **a person's capacity to maximize their own abilities, to successfully pursue one's purpose, yielding positive results for the individual and for others.** Each chapter in this book intends to serve as fuel for your fire as you actively strive toward greatness, by pursuing your purpose, not as a set destination but as a life-long journey.

Chapter 1

Education: The Key that Unlocks the Door

Greatness lies inside of you. Everyone is born to achieve and everyone can accomplish great things, especially when education is made a top priority. Not everyone can be famous, but everyone can be great, if that person maximizes his or her abilities. Academic goal-setting is an important key towards unlocking such greatness. Ask yourself, "What do I want to accomplish in school and in life?" Your goal may be to make the honor roll or become the first person in your family to graduate from high school and attend college. Whatever your educational goals are, it's important to realize that a goal that is unset often goes unmet. Be intentional about reaching academic excellence, develop an action plan or improvement strategies that will help you reach your goals and help to hold you accountable for your goals. What a disappointment to end your academic career thinking, "I could have achieved so much more, if I had truly applied myself."

It is important to recognize that your education is very important and how you pursue your academic career speaks monuments about you as a person. I refer to one's studies as their academic career, because it's your job to go to school and do your best while there. Your rewards and benefits will appear in various ways - by earning good grades, through self-improvement and by eventually reaching your career goals. For many, life without a high quality education is very difficult.

Set academic goals

What are your academic goals for this school year and what do you plan to accomplish? Be specific. Do you plan to make the honor roll, or finally bring up your math grade, or earn an academic scholarship for college? Whatever your goals, be sure to write them down and review them daily to serve as a constant reminder of the plans that you have established. I recently read a statistic showing only about 3% of the population, actually write down their goals. Something positive happens when we write down our goals. It gives us a sense of accountability and reminds us that we have something meaningful to aim for.

Develop an action plan that will help hold you accountable and work diligently toward reaching these goals. Get a vision for your academic career. Dream big and work hard! I suggest setting at least two academic goals per school year, along with an action plan for reaching these goals. Action plan means the specific steps or strategies that you will take in order to achieve your goals. A set of "I wills" might include for example, "I will ask more questions in class," "I will turn in my homework on time," or "I will study on a regular basis." These "I will" statements can also be considered as "I must" statements. Don't allow yourself any wiggle room or excuses that will block you from carrying out these declarations. Your success literally depends on it.

Maintain a positive attitude

It is often said that a person's attitude determines their altitude. I strongly agree with this principle, recognizing, however, that many students lack the confidence or do not have adequate support at home and these conditions, in turn, can generate negative attitudes. Perhaps you lack financial resources or struggle with emotional issues or with a learning disability. Whatever you may lack in one area of your life, be determined to make it up in another area. For example, where you may lack money or resources, make it up in motivation and creativity. If home stability is a problem, make it up in tenacity or work ethic and always try your best. Develop a "by any means necessary" attitude towards reaching academic excellence, as long as the means are positive.

The African slaves who were brought to America, who suffered mightily under the harsh conditions and abuse of slavery, serve as a great example of this "by any means necessary" approach to getting an education. Many of these individuals were so determined to be educated and learn to read and write that they created and organized *pit schools*. Pit schools were underground pits where slaves would risk their lives to sneak into at night to educate themselves and learn to read and write.

What would drive these individuals to risk their lives in order to learn and gain some education? They recognized that education was their ticket to freedom. Their education could not be beaten out of them; their education was the best gift that they could give to themselves and to future generations.

I challenge every young reader to garner strength from and enslaved people and be mindful of the importance of their education. I encourage you to approach each school day eager to learn, prepared to give undivided attention to the instruction that is available. If a person arrives at school with a lackadaisical or an "I don't care" attitude, his or her day will likely reflect it. Instead, approach each day with a positive attitude, eager to learn, recognizing that "Each time I learn something new, I grow as a person, and move one step closer towards reaching my goals." With this type of positive attitude, you will realize that many of the issues that you face can be managed and overcome. Here is a positive affirmation worth committing to memory:

"I am too hopeful to remain sad, too positive to be doubtful, and too determined to be defeated."

<u>Be willing to ask for help</u>

One of the best ways to help yourself academically, is to reach out for assistance, when needed. There is no shame in struggling. What is problematic is when a person needs help but is unwilling to ask for it. Problems are inevitable and some problems are unavoidable. This reality calls on us to be solution-minded. One way to determine if you are a solution-minded person is to ask yourself this question: In my daily conversations, do I find myself talking more about problems than possible solutions? We must always be ready and willing to tackle life's problems with a positive attitude, an open-mind and a strong desire to accomplish that which we have set out to achieve. A person's willingness, to ask for help is vital to finding the necessary solution(s). For example, if you are struggling in a particular subject area, be sure to ask your teachers, parents or a trusted adult for help. This may require staying after-school for additional help from a teacher or peer, asking more questions in class, or acquiring tutorial assistance outside of school. This support can go a long way towards improving your grades and subject mastery. The price for success is great, and the sacrifices significant. So how much do you want to be successful? If the answer is very much, then be willing to work hard for it! If you have been struggling or underachieving in school, step your game up and put in the necessary time. It's not too late to begin working up to your academic abilities.

Consistency is key; we become what we do consistently. If you are studying daily and with proper technique then success and positive results are just around the corner. However, if minimal effort is put forth, if the approach to learning is care-free, then the goal of producing positive academic results is merely wishful thinking. The journey to greatness is not painless, and you will experience setbacks along the way. Success requires a tremendous amount of time and sacrifice, but the sweet taste of success is well worth the time and energy that you exert. Just think, when you receive your high school diploma and your college degree, these will be clear indications of how your hard work has paid off!

    If for any reason you ask for help and don't receive the assistance that you are looking for, be sure to keep reaching out until you find the right source. Don't become discouraged if others do not go out of their way to assist you. Continue to reach out to different sources, to include parents, teachers, school counselors, principals or another trusted peer or adult. As you continue reaching out for help, eventually you will find the help that you are looking for. Become your own biggest and best educational advocate, you and your future are worth the investment!

Strategies for Academic success

- Make your education a top priority
- Arrive to school well rested and eager to learn
- Pay attention in class
- Take good notes
- Ask questions as needed
- Get and stay organized
- Be willing to stay after school for tutorial support

Helpful Study skills

- Commit to studying on a regular basis
- Study in an area conducive for learning
- Be willing to use a study partner
- Quiz yourself – Make flash cards
- Develop an afternoon/evening routine

Chapter 2

Character Matters

A person's character encompasses the core and essence of who we are as individuals; our personal attributes and characteristics. Character building is a vital element in becoming successful in life. Success is measured in many different ways. One person's definition of success may differ completely from another person's. Our experiences, values, goals and desires help to define our definition of success. A person can be a tremendous success in regards to their career, a sport or a hobby, but if their character won't sustain their talent or ability, then many times the success or accolades that a person garners can disappear or be placed in a serious jeopardy.

When we look at the "Great Recession" or financial crisis (that started towards the end of 2008) that the U.S and many other countries have experienced, we recognize that much of the devastation could have been avoided, if those in charge of the financial and banking industry had made sound judgment on sound information. Instead, what has been discovered is that financial risk taking and underhanded home lending practices greatly assisted in causing the global financial meltdown that will take years if not decades to recover from. The risky and sometimes illegal acts of some caused much harm to many. This is what can happen when appropriate character development does not take place; our society, our families and our institutions suffer as a whole. It's important to note that talent alone does not ensure success. Character also matters in a major way. Talent coupled with good character makes for a powerful combination.

How would you describe your character? What type of person are you striving to become? I hope that you are and strive to be a person of high (quality) character, a person who's dedicated to making wise decisions and willing to do what's right even when no one is watching. Our world is in desperate need of individuals of exemplary character everywhere - in every profession, every school and in every organization, to make certain that the world that our ancestors have left us is made better. We owe it to them, we owe it to ourselves, and we owe it to those who will come after us.

"Never allow your talent to take you to a place that your character won't sustain you"

Perhaps you know of someone personally or have heard of someone who has been in the public eye and who possessed tremendous talent and abilities, having gained much recognition or fame, but their character flaws greatly damaged them or caused them to lose what they worked so hard to achieve. These individuals may have strengthened their craft but neglected their character in some way. If character development is not made a top priority, this fate can happen to any of us.

Every person has strengths and weaknesses, and both of these deserve attention and self-examination in order to advance. This process is called personal growth and development. Just as it takes time and effort in order to increase physical endurance or build muscles, the process of character development takes time and effort; it's a life-long process that deserves much attention. Let's examine three essential character traits that must be developed in your pursuit of greatness.

Respect

I believe that respect is the foundation upon which good character is built. Self-respect and respect for others helps to position a person to carry out his or her purpose in life. Disrespect on the other hand, is a toxic character trait that hurts people, relationships and institutions, on all levels. When I conduct classroom lessons and ask students their definition of respect, students often reply by saying..."The Golden rule" or "Treat others the way that you wish to be treated." Many of the basic principles that we are taught as young children, still ring true. Showing respect and consideration for yourself and others is a character trait that will always serve you well.

I do recognize that many young people grow up in homes, go to schools, or live in neighborhoods where disrespect has overwhelmed their environment. Perhaps respect is not been adequately modeled or demonstrated for you. I challenge you to make a mental and a heart shift today and respect yourself as the valuable and worthwhile person that you are. I further challenge you to treat your parents/guardians, teachers and classmates with the respect, consideration and courtesy that you desire for yourself. I do realize that this task is made much more difficult when you are surrounded by disrespect; however, greatness is not reached with ease, but through perseverance and self-control. It's vitally important to realize that others are watching you and may follow your example. You may have a younger sibling or other relatives that look up to you. Perhaps you are their sole inspiration; resolve within yourself to be that positive example of respect.

    When I meet with families in crisis, I notice how the issue of disrespect is very often the root cause of their struggle. This disrespect usually leads to abuse in various forms and makes change seem nearly impossible for these families. Disrespect and abuse go hand in hand and create negative, toxic environments that usually explode in anger.

One of the first strategies that I begin to work on with families facing such issues is respect building. In homes where disrespect has become the norm, I seek to make the involved families aware that none of the other behavioral strategies that will be pursued will take full effect until a basic level of respect is built in the home. Families must agree to work hard at showing one another respect from the outset, through words and deeds. Anger is a universal emotion; everyone gets angry at times. Anger channeled in the right direction can produce positive results. For example, an angry person may decide to take a walk or spend time doing something productive as opposed to remaining in a heated argument. Unmanaged anger can destroy relationships and opportunities. Far too many individuals and families are filled with excessive anger and when this anger is not properly addressed, the consequences can be devastating to themselves and to others. Our overcrowded jails and prisons are proof positive of this fact.

The principle of respect building really resonated with one particular family that I was working with. For reasons of confidentiality, I will refer to this young man as Danny. Danny had been suspended from school repeatedly, for numerous offences. Danny struggles with emotional and psychological issues that usually results in him lashing out in anger towards classmates and adults; Danny also threatened to harm himself and others. His mother was at her absolute wit's end in dealing with his disrespectful and dangerous behavior that was often directed at her and Danny's two siblings. Early on, after I presented the principle and practices of respect building to this family in counseling, Danny's mother decided to adhere to this principle. She decided to stop using profanity and other disrespectful language in the home and to avoid escalating combative situations by lashing out in anger. She also began showing more consideration for Danny's and her other children's feelings. Remaining respectful in words and deeds when others are lashing out in anger can be very difficult; however Danny's mother remained consistent and faithful to this approach.

All though there have been setbacks along the way, this family continues to work through problems and has made steady progress. Danny's angry outbursts have decreased considerably in the home, his disciplinary record in school has improved, and he has made positive strides in dealing with his psychological and emotional state. Respect building in the home helped to lay the foundation for the other behavioral strategies to take effect. Danny's mother recognized that she was the only person that she could change, and the change in the home that she so desperately desired began with her.

This story highlights the fact that positive relationships should be built upon respect. Everyone longs for respect. Respect is rarely received until it is first given, and once a person gives respect they are much more likely to have it reciprocated. It is also very important for a person to respect and value him or herself as a person. Therefore, respect yourself by making wise choices that line up with your goals and values. Respect yourself in your choice of friends, and understand that making wise choices for yourself and your future will not always be popularly accepted. As you respect yourself and others, you will want to surround yourself with other like-minded, positive and successful people.

What actions will you take to show yourself more respect?

_____

_____

How can you show more respect for others?

_____

_____

Responsibility

    Responsibility is also a very important character trait in pursuit of greatness. If respect is the foundation upon which good character is built, then responsibility constitutes the walls and structures that keep the house standing. The wise proverb, "To whom much is given, much is required" puts this concept into perspective. Whether completing your class or homework, doing your chores, or participating in a sport or extracurricular activity; we all have responsibilities and obligations that must be met. They are a major part of growing up and maturing.

    As individuals, the more tasks and responsibilities that we take on, the more overwhelmed and stressed we can become. I recall having similar feelings during my seventh grade school year. This was the year where more was expected of me academically and organizationally. I really wanted to do well and perform up to my abilities, but the amount of coursework, homework and teacher expectations increased significantly. I remember coming home from school feeling overwhelmed with the amount of homework on my plate, to the point of tears, as I discussed these increased expectations with my father. My father listened to me, reassured me that things would be ok and encouraged me to continue to do my best. He was right, as the year went on, the more I began to improve my study habits the more I began to meet these increased expectations. The pull of wanting to hang out with friends began to subside, as I realized that I would simply have to tell my friends that I could not come outside to play, until my homework was completed. Looking back, I'm glad that I was tested in such a way. These obstacles and increased expectations helped to boost my confidence, proving to me that I could come out on top if I prioritized my time, disciplined myself and stepped up to meet the tasks before me. As you tackle your various responsibilities, you too may feel overwhelmed by the pressure that accompanies completing assignments and honoring commitments. Remember, the sacrifices that you make today and the commitments that you honor are not in vain; you are moving upward and onward toward your destiny. Don't get tired of doing the right things; the tests and obstacles that you face are preparing you for the future. Stay encouraged and committed, reminding yourself that your journey to success is not a sprint, but a marathon.

Avoid Burnout

Finding balance in life is essential on the road to success. Knowing when to get rest and when to accelerate your effort is paramount. It's very easy to get burned out when we take on too many obligations and activities. When we manage our time ineffectively and over-extend ourselves, it's common for people to lose the joy or passion of that particular area of interest. Outside influences or pressure that we put on ourselves can also lead to burnout. Stay fresh by reminding yourself of the original reason that led you to follow your interest. Maintain the love and joy for your activities and responsibilities by not overdoing them. If you are feeling burnout, allow yourself some time to miss the activity, and perhaps you will return to that activity more refreshed. You may decide to select a different activity that excites you more or decide to part ways from that activity.

    Over time, I've had the opportunity to speak with a number of students who had become burned out, having taken on too many activities at once. Most start off well, with very good intentions; however, when ambition and time-management do not meet, an imbalance is created which usually leads to burnout. For example, one student that I worked with spent 4-5 hours each night at gymnastics practice. This left her with very little time to complete her homework and time for friends, which then increased her overall stress level and performance in school. I offered this student and her parents' strategies for amending her afternoon schedule, which included informing the gymnastics coach that the student may need to take some afternoons off, or arrive at practice late in order to maintain a healthy life balance.

    A busy schedule can be a good thing, in that we should be actively engaged in bettering ourselves and the activities or organizations that we are apart of, but be sure to take time out for yourself - time for your studies and time for family and friends. The world needs you to be well balanced, rejuvenated and productive with the gifts, skills and attributes that make you unique. Be sure to not allow a sport or an activity, to dramatically deplete your energy, to the point where you are not giving adequate time to your studies and other responsibilities. Perhaps you should choose one or two sports or clubs to participate in, as opposed to three or four. Consider developing an afterschool schedule, as a way to prioritize your time and find balance.   Often times we want to have it all; however, we must recognize that we may not be able to have it all, at once. Pace yourself and place first things first, be willing to make some tough choices about your priorities. This will help you to maximize your potential and avoid burnout.

Ask yourself:

1. What are the most important tasks that I need to accomplish, at this time?
2. What is the timeline for my accomplishing this task?

3. Which tasks need to become secondary, while I accomplish my primary task?

Be sure to make time for:

- ✓ Yourself
- ✓ Your studies
- ✓ Family & friends
- ✓ Fun and leisure time
- ✓ Community and civic Involvement

Which priorities listed above deserve more of your attention, and what steps will you take to address them?

_____

_____

_____

Citizenship

Authentic greatness is made more real when individuals embrace true citizenship. One common characteristic seems to loom large amongst those inspirational historical figures that are largely considered to be great; that being their extraordinary sense of civic responsibility. These individuals seemed to serve a cause and purpose greater than themselves and desired to leave the world a better place than the way they found it. Some examples of great public servants and citizens are President John F. Kennedy, Dr. Martin Luther King Jr., Susan B. Anthony, Thomas Edison, Albert Einstein, Harriet Tubman, and Frederick Douglas; each used his or her own unique gifts to enhance our society in significant ways. Great citizens love and respect their country and are willing to serve it by serving others. An over-arching value that helps to make America such a great nation is the service and sacrifices made by its citizens. While financial and military power are key components to the strength of any nation, it's the sacrifices and contributions made from everyday citizens, both past and present, that undergird and build the foundation for the success that any nation ascends to. Through out America's history to include times of war and peace, during the woman's suffrage movement or the struggle for civil rights and equal treatment under the law for all; many citizens, young and old alike, from different ethnic backgrounds and various beliefs, have given so much to strengthen the democracy that we enjoy today.

    America is certainly not devoid of its issues and problems, as this county still has many problems that it must face and conquer. Equality and justice for all is truly a work in progress. However, there is little doubt as to why others from all over the globe have sought out, and still seek out, America as a place of hope, prosperity and as the land of opportunity. A spirit of toil and struggle has challenged and still challenges this nation to grapple with its identity and live up to the ideals that are so evident in its founding documents. In spite of all of our issues, America is still a country where dreams can still come true, especially when the belief in that dream is unwavering and tied to hard work and perseverance. It's important to recognize that the sacrifices and heroic deeds of our past and present countrymen did not and do not go unnoticed and are greatly appreciated. Be sure to thank those individuals who are on the front lines of making our country great, whether civilian or military. Freedom is not free. It comes with a heavy price and we all can contribute in our own way to making freedom more lasting for ourselves and for future generations. Not every person is called upon to make "the ultimate sacrifice," but everyone can serve our county in some capacity. Through acts of kindness, serving others in need, or giving your time and attention to public and civic matters, patriotism and civic responsibility can be demonstrated in many ways. If you feel an "urge to serve," but have not decided which role you will play as a contributing citizen, I encourage you to get in the game and take to heart the words of Mohandas Gandhi, the 20th Century, Indian Revolutionary and political figure:

> "The best way to find yourself, is to lose yourself in the service of others."

Service to others is one of the highest forms of citizenship. Something remarkable happens when people open up their heart and commit themselves to helping others. Whether donating food or clothing to those in need, helping out an elderly person, or assisting at an animal shelter, there are sundry ways to empower and serve your community. If you are actively involved in some form of service, your community thanks you. Keep up the good work! You are truly making a difference. Your example and commitment to the betterment and up-build up of others can cause a chain reaction of acts of kindness in your community and beyond. It's amazing … the more you serve and empower others the more empowered you begin to feel. Service enables individuals to become a part of the world's solutions instead of its problems. By being well-informed and service-oriented, you have the power to make significant change.

Classwork:

In what ways can you better serve others and your community?

_____

_____

Chapter 3

Family Matters

Another true measure of greatness can be found through family success. A famous American educator and psychiatrist Rudolph Dreikurs pointed out, that the primary need for a child is the need for belonging. Family success may be the most challenging and yet the most rewarding goal to attain. The importance of family can never be overstated. The family unit is one of the most important places to find belonging. Family has a profound impact on us and helps to shape our character and future. It's safe to safe to say, that there are no perfect families because every family has issues and problems. In families where there is no great sense of love or belonging, children often search for belonging in other places, many times the wrong places. For example, if a young person is having trouble at home and is having a tough time getting along with their parents and relatives, it may entice that youngster to associate more closely with others who may positively or negatively influence them, depending on the maturity, mindset and environment of the individual involved.

Perhaps you have little to no connection with your family, and may be wondering, how you can build or re-establish unity. I won't pretend that I know exactly how you feel or that there is a quick fix to the situation. Moving forward from family hurt or abandonment can be an enormous task, but it can be done. It's important to point out that family comes in different shapes and sizes. Maybe your family includes your foster family or members of the network of friends that you've made or those individuals that have evolved into family. If you are struggling to find a sense of family, I encourage you to open up your heart and be willing to reach out to those individuals that love and care for you and adopt them as your family. Where there are broken ties in your family, work to reconcile them (if possible).

Choosing to forgive others is one of the best ways to begin down the road to recovery. It's important to note that not all recovery includes reconnection. For example, you may need to forgive a person that is deceased or forgive a person that is not asking for forgiveness. Forgiveness does not excuse or condone bad behavior, abuse, neglect or abandonment that you may have experienced. Choosing to forgive others can begin the healing process that you desire. Bitterness and "un-forgiveness" can take on lives of their own and have negative physical, emotional and relational effects on you. Forgiveness allows you to move into your destiny minus the baggage of vengeance and animosity that "un-forgiveness" brings. Choosing to forgive says "I'm not going to allow the negative events that have happened to me, block my future or stop me from finding and living out my purpose." "I choose to forgive; I refuse to see myself as a victim, but as a victor." Forgiving others is not always an easy choice, and for some the process can take some time, but you should recognize that forgiveness is a choice that will benefit you and others.

Life and its various obstacles can tear away at the fabric of family. In the hustle and bustle of our daily lives, it's easy to get pulled away from family and lose those important connections. Work to develop and maintain your family connections by spending time with your family, and by starting or trying to maintain family traditions or outings like family reunions. Family should help and support one another through the numerous trials and triumphs of life. When we disconnect and or distance ourselves from family, we suffer and the family unit that is intended to be strong is made weaker. Wherever there are broken ties in your family, work to repair and reconnect where possible, you will be doing yourself and your family a big favor.

<u>Communicate with family</u>

Communication is critical to any successful relationship. In friendships, interactions with teachers, co-workers, and certainly within the family unit, communication is the glue that holds these important connections together. It's virtually impossible to develop and maintain a lasting relationship with the absence of effective communication. It's important to note that communication is a two way street that involves talking and listening. For many, talking comes more easily while listening is more difficult. **Reflective**

listening involves active listening, demonstrated by attentive body language and your ability to reflect back to the speaker what you heard them say. Using this technique can certainly improve your communication skills. Be sure to talk with your parents or guardians about what's going on in your life. I do recognize that many young people reach an age when hanging out and spending time with their parents is not cool. Believe it or not, your parents may be able to offer much insight and wisdom on how to handle many of life's circumstances or at least offer a set of listening ears. Show interest in your parents as well, by asking them about their day and inquiring about their childhood and upbringing, and asking probing questions about your family history. You might be amazed at all of the valuable nuggets and insight you can learn about yourself, your parents, relatives and your family history. As you begin to show more interest in your parents and their values, listen to what they have to say; the lines of communication within your family will be improved. Far too often, the lines of communication within families are closed. This distance and isolation ends up hurting individuals and relationships inside and outside of the home. Resolve to actively combat these negative trends in your family by working to become a more effective communicator.

As a maturing person and as an emerging leader you can take steps towards closing any distance within your home. By opening up and demonstrating a willingness to communicate more effectively, you can take the lead in this process. It's extremely difficult to solve problems within the home or anywhere else for that matter, when effective communication is lacking or when critical issues are ignored or swept under the rug. Not all problems are inevitable; some of issues that ail our families can be addressed through effective communication.

Effective communicators should be:

1. Quick to listen (attentive listening)

2. Slow to speak (give thought to your response, before speaking)

3. Slow to anger (manage your emotions by not allowing your emotions to control you)

Family meetings are designated times when families come together to discuss family concerns in a safe and loving environment. Family meetings can go a long way towards enhancing communication, solving problems and strengthening family bonds, especially when some basic ground rules are set and when each family member's opinions and ideas are valued. These family meetings should take place at least 2-4 times per month, lasting approximately 15-30 minutes per meeting, based upon the needs of each family. Some families need more intense interventions in order to address more deep seated issues and may even require professional counseling. With a positive attitude and a strong willingness to reconnect and communicate with your family, you can find common ground that can lead to a more cohesive family unit.

Self-esteem and Friendships

One of the coolest parts of the adolescent years are times spent with family and friends; experiencing new opportunities and the excitement of gaining new freedoms, such as driving or getting an after-school job. The teen years can also be some of the most confusing and challenging. Many struggle with trying to fit in with peers and deal with the increased expectations that are placed on them, by the adults in their lives. Add to that, the issues and pressures that heavily come into play surrounding self-esteem or self-image. Self-esteem: how a person feels about him or her self, their self-worth. Scores of young people struggle with the added stress that comes along with the increased pressure by friends and associates; many find it very difficult to recover from such struggles, even well into their adult life. The pressure to experiment with drugs, alcohol, sex, gangs, and other behaviors during this stage of life is real and can be relentless.

One way of handling the increased pressure placed on you by your peers, is to be actively involved in positive activities. I call this being "too busy to get into trouble." As individuals, I believe we should be so actively involved in positive activities that we don't have time to get distracted with harmful behaviors that ultimately lead to dashed hopes and dreams. When you get a glimpse of your future and get actively plugged into the causes and activities that are at your disposal, the alternative of getting caught-up into destructive behaviors and the negative consequences that follow, absolutely pale in comparison. For example, jail or college, which would you choose?

I do recognize that part of a teenager's job is to push the boundaries, try new things and have fun. I would add one more description to a teenager's job, and that is - *don't mess up so badly during your adolescent years that you can't recover later*. For example, one night of excessive drinking and getting behind the wheel can result in a lifetime of harm and devastation.

The second principle for handling peer pressure is accomplished through the practice of applying **positive peer-pressure**. So how does this work? Glad you asked. Well, when a friend or peer attempts to persuade you to do something wrong or something that could jeopardize your future, simply attempt to persuade them to do the right thing! Put the pressure on them to make wise choices that will help their future; this will shift your posture from defensive to offensive. For example, let's say a friend or peer is trying to convince you to skip school to smoke marijuana. You could apply the same amount of energy (or more) to the situation by challenging your friend to remain in school with you; this choice will help your friend's chances of graduating from school on time and moving on in life. If your friend refuses to make smart choices, over a period of time, it's worth evaluating whether or not this friendship is built to last. Applying positive peer-pressure not only enhances your leadership skills, it also helps in taking you off of the hot seat. It can also put pressure on your peers to better themselves and make wiser decisions.

Two ways of handling peer pressure:

- Positive Involvement – "Too busy to get into trouble"
- Apply Positive Peer-Pressure

I remember, during my early teenage years spending a lot of time with my friend and next door neighbor Deon. Deon and I played sports together, spent time at one another's house, and even started our own lawn mowing business, in the neighborhood. Deon was a good friend; he was good natured, energetic, and lots of fun to be around. As I look back, I realize that Deon had numerous personal and family struggles that I believe took a serious toll on his self-esteem. These issues played out in his behavior, in and outside of school.

Many people struggle with having low self-esteem. Living in a society that places so much value on physical appearance, material objects and popularity can create tremendous pressure, especially on young people. As a pre-teenager, I can recall moments when I struggled with my own self-confidence, which prohibited me from trying out new things. I was one of the youngest students in my grade level; I lacked some of the experience and seasoning that many of my peers had. In retrospect, I can see how these experiences worked in my favor and challenged me to become a better person. I also attribute faith, family and community support as being major factors in my growth process. I don't know that my friend Deon had this same support. At the time, Deon never really expressed his feelings to me, but I could tell by his withdrawal and mood swings that he was struggling. Deon had a rocky relationship with his step-father, and I don't believe Deon had a relationship with his biological father. Some of the issues and tension that Deon had with his stepfather were evident and personally weighed on him. Although Deon struggled with some of his peer relationships, he always seemed to manage to pull himself together and get back on track. My friend Deon was searching for something; he wanted to find his place in the world and contribute to society, in a positive way. No matter how many times he was knocked down, he always seemed to pick himself up, dust himself off and try again. Deon's resiliency, his ability to bounce back from difficulty is an enduring quality that I remember about him most.

Deon eventually moved out of the neighborhood and we lost contact as friends. Occasionally I would run into his younger sister and she would inform me that he was the same old Deon, still getting knocked down and still getting back up. This childhood friendship had a significant impact on me and impressed upon me the idea that *we can't always control what happens to us in life, but we can control our response to what happens.*

I hope that Deon found some small measure of consolation in our friendship. I wonder if I could I have been a better friend to Deon and provided more support to him as he dealt with personal and family problems. As I think back on this experience, it serves as additional fuel to my fire to continue doing my part in helping to build others' esteem, and not tear it down. It's important to recognize that we may never know exactly what our family members, friends or acquaintances are experiencing. Yet through words or deeds we can be a great source of encouragement to help them along the way. We could easily find ourselves in need or in a similar predicament at some point.

Perhaps you find yourself struggling with low self-esteem, trying to find your place in the world. Maybe you don't feel like you have what it takes to become successful. I encourage you to be your own best friend and biggest cheerleader and recognize that self-worth cannot be measured by appearance or by material possessions. You may have characteristics that you would like to see changed, this is typical. I encourage you to act on the things that are in your control. For example, suppose you wish to lose weight to help improve your self-esteem. By making healthier eating choices and with exercise, you can take positive steps toward boosting your self-confidence. If you lack confidence due to continual hurtful remarks that have been hurled at you or from negative experiences from your past, a better option may include seeking counseling or therapy, in dealing with these unresolved issues. Always take positive steps towards self-improvement, even if these changes take a while and even if you experience setbacks along the way. Never give up on yourself or your future. Recognize that you are valuable, significant and worthwhile.

    Negative thinking is one of the biggest obstacles to success. Be intentional about maintaining a positive attitude with the words that you speak about yourself (self-affirmation) and with the constructive actions that follow. Surround yourself with optimistic and progressive people, and seek out nurturing environments that will spark your intellect and curiosity to bring out the best in you. Remove the negative messages that may be playing in your mind and replace them with positive ones. Every time someone tells you what you can't do, or what you will never accomplish, follow up these discouraging statements with positive ones. Wake up every day and tell yourself, "I accept myself, I am special, I matter, and I am worthwhile." Remind yourself that you have what it takes to become successful, and that every day you are taking positive steps towards reaching your goals.

Recognize that you must take charge of the process for self-improvement and take ownership of your attitude and actions. Not everyone that you will encounter in life will feel giddy about you in your pursuit of greatness; unfortunately some individuals decide to boost their self-image by bullying or belittling others. At least there will be one person always in your corner looking out for your best interests and encouraging you, and that person is you. Don't let the negative energy, words, or actions of others block you from reaching your goals in life. Use their words or actions as stepping stones to success. **Great and successful individuals decide to use everything that happens to them in life (positive or negative) as motivation towards success.** You have the power to change and to improve, regardless of what you may be facing. It's going to require high self-esteem and self-confidence in order to accomplish all that is set before you. You have the gifts, talent, and the ability to make success a reality; make sure you have the proper attitude and outlook as well.

Please reflect on the following self-esteem building strategies:

- o Recognize that self-esteem matters (it will play out in how you treat others and how you allow others to treat you)

- Surround yourself with positive and progressive people
- Do not join in with others that attempt to belittle or devalue you
- Be your own best friend; speak positive words of encouragement to yourself
- Set positive goals for yourself and work diligently to achieve them

Questions:

1. What can you do to strengthen your family connections?

   _____

   _____

2. On a scale of 1 to 10, with 1 being very low, how would you rate your self-esteem?

   _____

3. What steps will you to take to improve your self-esteem and self-confidence?

   _____

   _____

Chapter 4

Career Planning

It's never too early to start planning for your career. Some people know very early in life what they wish to pursue as a career; for others it takes some time and a considerable amount of planning to discover their path. What career do you see yourself working in? Even if you don't know the answer to this question, it's neither too soon nor too late to start preparing.

Consider these four critical factors as you explore your career path:

1. Choose a career that you will be passionate about;
2. Match your skills and abilities to your career choice;
3. Prepare to make a positive impact throughout your career, and
4. Be certain your career choice will support you financially.

Passion (Factor 1)

When choosing a career path, passion should be a major motivating factor. Think about it -- you actually get to choose your career! What a golden opportunity. What career would you choose, even if you didn't get paid to do it? In other words, if all of your financial needs were met and if you could maintain a lifestyle

what you are good at doing, are not always one and the same. For example, I enjoy playing basketball, but this certainly does not mean that I possess the skill level needed to play professionally. This is why it's central to know your strengths and weaknesses in order to ensure that your skill level and area of passion match your career choice. When skill and passion meet at an intersection, then excellence and success are well within reach, especially when you include a strong work ethic.

   Are you gifted in the areas of math, science and literature? Perhaps your areas of strength are in the creative arts, technology, or you possess the gift of hospitality? Whatever skills and attributes that you possess, your area of gifting should be cultivated and enhanced in order to propel you toward your career aspirations. Be sure to develop a strong competency in the areas of language arts and math. All school subjects are important, but math and language arts are particularly important as they are two core subjects that will lay the foundation for academic achievement in all other subject areas. The US unemployment rate has been particularly high, post "The Great Recession" of 2008; yet there is an employment shortage in many high skilled, technical careers. Those students that excel in math and science will be in a great position to move into many of these prized, good-paying jobs. As our work force becomes increasingly competitive

craftsmanship and attention to detail, that abounds with creativity and fruitfulness? Try imagining your career as the latter, a beautiful and lasting tapestry of artwork and skill that is fully on display for all to see. Perhaps you will be the nurse or surgeon that always goes above and beyond for their patients or the scientist or engineer that's constantly striving to make advances in their field. Maybe you will be the teacher, firefighter or mechanic who so willingly gives much time and talent to others. Whatever your career choice or career path, let there be lasting images of the people that you have met and served, causes that you have championed, and positive results that you helped produced, through years of dedication and hard work. Let it be said and felt that the world and your profession are better off, because you were involved. As you pursue your career of choice, recognize that every profession is a people profession, because every career, in some form or another, affects people. The impact of your job performance will not only be measured by performance evaluations and bonuses earned, but also by the legacy and impact that you leave with people.

Practical steps for making a positive career impact:

1. Choose to be happy – I've heard it said that happiness is a choice. Whenever a nation faces difficult economic times, there is often a tendency to be overly negative or cynical in our thinking. Especially, when we turn on the television to hear news reports and even experience how the middle class in this country is

2. Volunteer – In the workplace, efficiency and production are crucial. When a worker's goal is to find ways to avoid tasks or responsibilities, the chances of this person being successful in their career is greatly decreased. One way to fight the instinct to cut corners and maximize your production is to develop a *strong volunteering spirit*. When you extend yourself to help others and assist them with a project or an assignment, you may be surprised at how you can constructively affect a work environment. Be willing to step "outside the box" and present creative ideas and assistance that will help make someone else's project or task a success. In the process, teamwork and trust will be established amongst colleagues, and this can help turn your team into a winning team. Don't shy away from taking on a leadership role as a volunteer within your organization. Taking such initiative will demonstrate to others that you are willing to step up to make the group better. It shows that you are a team player which can only help you advance in your career. It's astonishing to witness all of the things a winning team can accomplish when the vision is clear and the goals and expectations are high. This strong spirit of volunteerism will not only help you grow you as a person and as a professional, it also increases the likelihood that others will step up to help you when you are in need of assistance. A strong volunteer spirit can dramatically transform any working environment and spread like wildfire. Productivity and efficiency grow tremendously, when individuals role up

Earning Capacity (Factor 4)

Last but not least, the final career question for contemplation deals with the issue of money. Earning capacity is an important factor when choosing a career. After all, we all need careers that will support our physical needs and allow us to meet our financial obligations. However, if a person chooses a career based solely on its earning capacity and fails to include the other three aforementioned factors, (passion, skill and impact) the chances of that person becoming disgruntled and unproductive in their career are greatly increased.

The following chart from the United States Bureau of Labor Statics (2010) gives a clear indication of how educational attainment relates to the unemployment rate and earning capacity.

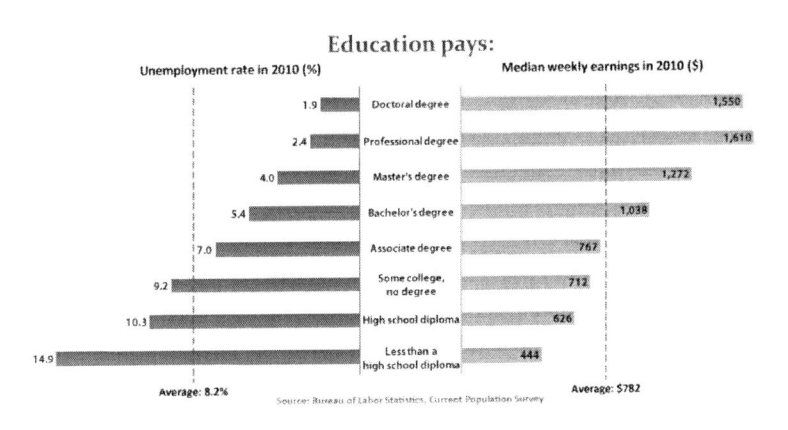

Education pays:

Unemployment rate in 2010 (%)	Education	Median weekly earnings in 2010 ($)
1.9	Doctoral degree	1,550
2.4	Professional degree	1,610
4.0	Master's degree	1,272
5.4	Bachelor's degree	1,038
7.0	Associate degree	767
9.2	Some college, no degree	712
10.3	High school diploma	626
14.9	Less than a high school diploma	444

Average: 8.2%   Average: $782

Source: Bureau of Labor Statistics, Current Population Survey

These statistics show that the unemployment rate rises and average weekly earnings significantly

Chapter 5

Strengthen your Spiritual Core

It is widely believed that human beings are composed of three basic components: mind, body and soul. We feed our physical bodies with food that gives us nourishment, and we feed our minds by gaining knowledge in various ways. It's imperative to realize that just as our minds and bodies need nourishment, so does the soul. The Miriam Webster dictionary gives the following definition of the soul: 1. the spiritual principle embodied in human beings, all rational and spiritual beings, or the universe, 2. the moral and emotional nature of human beings.

Have you ever asked yourself, "Why am I here on earth" or "What is my purpose in life?" These questions deal with the soulful or spiritual aspect of our lives which can easily go unnoticed and unnourished. I believe that a person can never truly be great until they are willing to be spiritually or morally great. A person can be physically strong, even educated at the finest academic institutions, yet if a person is emotionally, morally or spiritually bankrupt, then they will never fully actualize their true potential.

comfortable or convenient. For example, it would have been convenient for Dr. Martin Luther King Jr. not to join the civil rights movement, at the time he decided to do so. Dr. King had earned his Doctoral Degree, by the age of 26; he could have lived a successful and prosperous life based upon his educational attainment and hard work. Instead, Dr. King decided to risk his life to enter the movement for civil rights and take on the leadership role in the Montgomery Bus boycott of 1955. Dr. King realized early on in his life that his purpose was connected to the spiritual and moral liberation of the nation. The civil rights movement and fight for equality in the United States of America is a prime example of persons and a movement living in active pursuit of purpose, accomplishing great things. With the scars to show, our nation and society is more righteous and just due to their tireless work and sacrifices.

"The ultimate measure of a man is not where he stands in moments of comfort or convenience, but where he stands in times of challenge and controversy."
Rev. Dr. Martin Luther King, Jr.

Can a person ever truly attain spiritual greatness? I'm not sure, but in one's quest for spiritual greatness, a person can define his or her sense of purpose, grow and mature into an excellent human being, and make the lives of others better in the process.

With scores of young people dropping out of school at alarming rates (over 8% according to the U.S.

uninterrupted devotional time with the intention of connecting with God while gaining strength throughout the process. Mediation and self-reflection can also allow time for people to clear their minds and pause in contemplation. In our fast paced lives it can be difficult to quiet our minds, allow time to recalibrate our spiritual or moral compasses and self-reflect. Yoga can also help facilitate this process. Consider devoting at least 10 minutes per day for quiet time of prayer, meditation or reflection; it can pay tremendous dividends and help to recharge your spiritual battery.

2. Read Spiritual or Self-Help Books - So much can be learned from reading books like the Holy Bible, The Torah and The Koran. These books help feed our spirits and provide insight and governance for our lives. These, along with other self-help books give shining examples of men and women of faith that teach and inspire us to continue our journey toward spiritual greatness. Invest in yourself and strengthen your spiritual core by reading materials that are inspirational, and that challenge you to live your best life.

3. Study the lives of Spiritual and Moral Leaders – One of the great blessings of being an American citizen is the fact that we can openly practice or choose not to practice our religious beliefs. Reading and learning about great spiritual and moral leaders, both past and present, is a useful way to strengthen your spiritual and

and social change. While Mohandas Gandhi did hold elected office for a time, Dr. King did not; yet, both were able to use spiritual principles, moral reasoning and civil disobedience as weapons of love & justice that helped free the oppressed and the oppressors in their respective nations.

Dr. King offered the following words, during his 1963 eulogy of the four girls that died in the bombing of the Sixteenth Street Baptist Church in Birmingham, Alabama:

"God has a job for us to do. Maybe our mission is to save the soul of America. We can't save the soul of this nation throwing bricks. We can't save the soul of this nation getting our ammunitions and going out shooting physical weapons. We must know that we have something much more powerful. Just take up the ammunition of love." MLK

and others in the right direction. If you are setting a positive example for a younger sibling, then you are leading. Every time you get up and arrive at school or to work on time, you are leading. If you choose to help a person in need or, conversely, sit by and watch someone else being bullied or being taken advantage of, you are leading or setting an example by action or inaction. Let's commit to lead through positive actions.

Let's examine 7 key characteristics of a Highly Effective Leader (HEL)

Highly Effective Leaders:

1. Have Vision – In order to become a leader that operates at a high level, a person must see him or herself as a leader. For many, the idea or notion of

in helpful action. The willingness to serve does not place a person in a position of weakness; rather it demonstrates immense strength and epitomizes the essence of authentic leadership. When leaders see themselves as chief servants, they are more apt to inspire others to also serve, which is beneficial to the purpose that you are serving. It's important to note that HEL's are servant leaders who seek to serve others, not just be served by others.

   Some people maintain the view that leaders should always be out front giving orders, moving others into action, taking on an authoritative role. There are times when a HEL will need to do these things; however HEL's should also be ready to roll up their sleeves, get their hands dirty, and do what's necessary to enhance team cohesion and productivity. Some leaders take a more permissive approach toward leadership, believing they will be successful by simply giving in to the demands of others, unwilling to deal with conflicts that arise. This style of leadership rarely leads to success. Not all leaders have the responsibilities of an executive, a director or a supervisor. It's important to recognize that many leaders work more behind the scenes and may be more passive by nature, yet they are able to inspire others to operate at a high level, **leading by example**. As an emerging leader, be willing to take a more balanced approach, setting high expectations yet providing your team the means, motivation and tools necessary to be successful. Think about how much

undermined due to integrity issues or lack of consistency. It's important to say what you mean and be firm in your convictions. Most of the people that you work alongside will greatly appreciate your honesty because it will allow them to do their jobs better. People are more willing to forgive mistakes when they believe your motives are honest and sincere. They are much more eager to embrace a shared-vision and follow when the leadership is bold and operates with integrity. In every arena of your life, be committed to establishing cooperative working relationships that are built upon respect.

4. Are life-long learners – Highly Effective Leaders have an insatiable appetite for knowledge. They seek to grow personally and desirous of seeing others advance. People who serve in leadership capacities can become complacent or stagnant, especially when others are responsible for answering to them. An HEL postures themselves as a life-life long students, keeping an open mind regarding the ideas, concepts and strategies of others. Life-long learners see each day as an opportunity to learn more, teach more, and actively pursue their purpose. Never become complacent or stagnant with your current level of knowledge; there is always more to learn and to accomplish. Surround yourself with other "hungry" individuals that bring out the best in you, and that bring creative ideas and possible solutions to bear. One major responsibility of an HEL is to ***help set a positive tone for success*** that can

people can often be resistant to change and may seek to do things as they've always been done. People may say things like, "We've never done it that way." or "What's the point of changing?" Inspirational leaders seize these moments as opportunities to teach, pointing out that new heights are often reached through a forward moving mindset and practices. How and when this message is delivered requires skill and tact by those in leadership. Operating as a cohesive unit inspired by performance and teamwork is a worthwhile and attainable goal. Highly Effective Leaders recognize the importance of being transparent and consistently work to create an atmosphere of excellence through inspirational words and performance. One enormous test of leadership is in getting others to recognize the untapped potential that lies inside of them and fully appreciate how this potential is relevant to the overall success of the group or organization. HEL's must embody this "can do" attitude and assume the responsibility of becoming "Inspirer-in-Chief."

6. Solve-Problems - Highly Effective Leaders are problem-solvers and have a unique ability to perform their best under pressure. Highly Effective leaders are realistic in their approach toward problem-solving and view problems as opportunities to find solutions. A major responsibility that a HEL must assume is the need to guide themselves and others to deal with reality. So often when problems arise, there is a tendency to either minimize them or exaggerate them. HEL's get to the

This open atmosphere gives contributing members space to point out the things that are working well, raise the concerns or problems that need to be addressed, and suggest possible solutions.
Accountability is also critical because people don't always do what is expected, but what is inspected. This is why leaders should seek to hold themselves and others accountable for the shared goals and vision of the group at-large.

Here are some basic problem-solving principles to consider and apply:

Effective Problem-Solving

- Identify the problem
- Examine all facets of the problem (the contributing factors)
- Brainstorm possible solutions and explore alternatives
- Choose an alternative
- Apply the alternative (s)
- Allow time for the solution to work (closely monitor the situation)
- Be willing to revisit possible solutions and alternatives (if the desired result is not reached)

7. Produce Positive Results – Highly Effective Leaders must produce positive results. A leader can display exemplary character, possess the ability to inspire

further develop your character, strengthen your family ties, make career plans, strengthen your spiritual core and work toward becoming a Highly Effective Leader. Your passion for greatness will be well within your grasp and you will scale heights of success that can surpass your hopes and dreams. My goal is to encourage you along your journey, to realize that greatness is not a destination but *a journey* that must be actively pursued. Remember, you were Born to Achieve!